TRANSFER

TRANSFER

POEMS BY

NAOMI SHIHAB NYE

AMERICAN POETS CONTINUUM SERIES, NO. 128

BOA EDITIONS, LTD. ◦ ROCHESTER, NY ◦ 2011

First Edition
11 12 13 14   7 6 5 4 3 2 1

For information about permission to reuse any material from this book please
contact The Permissions Company at www.permissionscompany.com or e-mail
permdude@eclipse.net.

Publications by BOA Editions, Ltd.—a not-for-profit corpo-
ration under section 501 (c) (3) of the United States Internal
Revenue Code—are made possible with funds from a variety
of sources, including public funds from the New York State
Council on the Arts, a state agency; the Literature Program
of the National Endowment for the Arts; the County of Mon-
roe, NY; the Lannan Foundation for support of the Lannan
Translations Selection Series; the Mary S. Mulligan Charitable
Trust; the Rochester Area Community Foundation; the Arts
& Cultural Council for Greater Rochester; the Steeple-Jack
Fund; the Ames-Amzalak Memorial Trust in memory of Henry Ames, Semon
Amzalak and Dan Amzalak; and contributions from many individuals nationwide.
See Colophon on page 128 for special individual acknowledgments.

ART WORKS.
arts.gov

State of the Arts

NYSCA

Cover Design: Daphne Morrissey
Interior Design and Composition: Richard Foerster
Manufacturing: McNaughton & Gunn
BOA Logo: Mirko

Library of Congress Cataloging-in-Publication Data

Nye, Naomi Shihab.
  Transfer : poems / by Naomi Shihab Nye. — 1st ed.
    p. cm. — (American poets continuum series ; no. 128)
  ISBN 978-1-934414-52-1 (pbk. : alk. paper) — ISBN 978-1-934414-64-4
(hardcover : alk. paper)
  I. Title.
PS3564.Y44T73 2011
811'.54—dc23
                          2011025282

BOA Editions, Ltd.
250 North Goodman Street, Suite 306
Rochester, NY 14607
www.boaeditions.org
A. Poulin, Jr., Founder (1938–1996)

In Loving Memory of Our Father, Aziz Shihab

سلام

Aziz

Our father
who was always our father
not always our father

Refugee
not always
once a confident schoolboy
strolling Jerusalem streets

He knew the alleyways
spoke to stones
All his life he would pick up stones
and pocket them
On some he drew
faces

What do we say in the wake of one
who was always homesick?
Are you home now?
Is Palestine peaceful in some dimension
we can't see?
Do Jews and Arabs share the table?
Is holy in the middle?

Contents

Introduction   11

I

History   17
1935   18
Bats   19
I Don't Know   20
Scared, Scarred, Sacred   21
Haunted   24
Valley   25
Storyteller   26

II
"Just Call Me Aziz"
11 POEMS—TITLES BY AZIZ SHIHAB—FROM HIS NOTEBOOKS

Everything in Our World Did Not Seem to Fit   29
My Life Before America Had No Toilet Tissue   30
We Did Not Have Drinking Water in the Middle
    of the Ocean   31
Is Misery Near Kansas, I Asked   32
Many Asked Me Not to Forget Them   33
A Kansas Preacher Called Me Muscleman   34
I Hate It, I Love It   35
When One Is So Far from Home, Life Is a Mix
    of Fact and Fiction   36
Being Back with the Family Is Quite Wonderful
    but Terribly Exhausting   37
Member of the Tribe   38
Fifty Years Since I Prayed or Thought in Arabic   39

III

Knowing   43

Dusk   44

Thirsty   45

Amir & Anna   46

Mall Aquarium, Dubai   47

"The Only Democracy in the Middle East"   48

War   49

Maximum Security   51

Remembering William Stafford   52

The Burn   53

Strict   54

Real Estate   55

Tiny Cucumbers   56

Swerve   57

Where Are You Now?   58

Archive   60

Won't You Still Love Me When I'm Dead?   62

Hello, Palestine   63

For Aziz, Who Loved Jerusalem   64

Undone   65

Love You   Love You   Love You   66

Sandhill Cranes at the Platte River   67

IV

THIS YEAR, I'LL WRITE WITH ASH

Alive   71

Moment   72

The Young Poets of Winnipeg   73

What Will Happen?   74

Morning Birds   75

Lying While Birdwatching   77

Where Were We?   78

Dear Mediator   79

Eye Contact with a Squirrel   80

Family Love   81
You Are Wanted in the Office   82
Dallas   83
Muscat Sundown   84
Burlington, Vermont   85
For Mutanabbi Street   86
Mystery   87
Endure   88

V

CROSSING THE CREEK

Later   91
Window   92
Savigny Platz   93
Footstool   96
Bleibtreustrasse 31   97
Last Wishes   98
Ringing   99
Call to Prayer   100
Cinco de Mayo   101
Chicho Brothers Fruit & Vegetable #1   102
Chicho Brothers Fruit & Vegetable #2   103
Frankly   104
Father's Day   105
We Can't Lose   106
Mom Gives Away Your Ties   107
WAR is RAW Backwards & Forwards   108
Able to Say It   109
Comfort   111
"Bees see your face as a strange flower."   112
At the Block Island Ferry   113
Wavelength   115

Acknowledgments   121
About the Author   123
Colophon   128

TRANSFER

Introduction

...then I will begin with you that hesitant conversation going on and on and on.

—Alastair Reid, "My Father, Dying"

My father wanted us to write a book together. A "dialogue," he called it. But he kept sending me monologues by e-mail and fax. Rants on topics I'd heard him discuss many times—frustrations, difficulties, peculiarities of a long life-in-exile. Perspectives on this and that.

He was already on dialysis. I would have done anything he wanted.

I tried to respond to what he sent, but he'd send another monologue instead. He wouldn't answer questions. There was no continuity.

So what is a dialogue, Dad? I asked. Where is the back and forth?

You're letting me down, he wrote. You're not doing it right. I want to do it, but you're refusing.

There was no thread.

So now he's immigrated again, to a country beyond sight, and I keep talking. Two weeks after he died I carried a stack of incomplete notebooks from his messy office to my messy office.

Now what? I said. Can you hear me? Are you anywhere? I'll type up some of your lines, your spare and elegant English longhand, and see if—anything answers. It may not work but I'm thinking about how—what can I do?—became your anthem.

It was the empty cup you held out with a trembling hand.
Something might come along.

It's not so much that I want him still here for me. It's that I can't
stand the thought of the world without him in it.

He loved the world. The world frustrated him endlessly, but he
loved it and hoped for it.
He'd step out of his bedroom each morning with flair, as if onto
a stage. Freshened face, clean shirt.
Hello my friend! to people he encountered. I wonder now if this
were his method for deflecting possible racism or rejection. *Hello
friend!* to every waitress and shoe salesman. We argued with him
when we were kids. Dad, you don't even *know* her.
Well, she'll be my friend faster if I say that.

When the *Midwest Quarterly* invited me to submit a series of
poems, I thought of how my father had first immigrated to the
American Midwest in 1951 as a college student, and used some
of his notebook lines as titles, thinking I would write the poems
which followed. The little series "Just Call Me Aziz" emerged in
his voice, however. So, it still wasn't a dialogue.

When we were kids, he couldn't stand to see anyone sick. Once
when my brother vomited beside the Mississippi River, our
father, comforting him, vomited too.

Who would ever have guessed a vibrant skinny man of optimism
and energy, who disliked all medical procedures, would end
of having heart attacks, diabetes, kidney failure, dialysis? He
pricked his finger to check his blood sugar for years. He grew
comfortable with bleeding.

Why do you have diabetes, Grandpa?
I think because I used to put sugar in my coffee.

Missing him contains moments so intense I don't know how
I will continue. Pause on the path, stricken, then his love and
humor speak to me again and I move forward, soothed.

His words about the wars in Iraq and Afghanistan were concise
and simple:
GET OUT.
AMERICANS GET OUT.
People would begin to counter ...*but what about...*
And he would say, GET OUT! What are we doing there really?
We need to get out!

He never cursed. The worst I ever heard him say was *Bozos*.

As for his own conflicted first land? He never gave up hope.
Everything depended on mutual respect. The sadness of my
father was a landmass under water.

I

History

In the 15th century, the sailor Ahmed Bin Majed,
wrote about movements of stars,
sang praises to the moon and the waves.

Today, millions of people
crammed into cities,
selling fruits from rickety carts.

It's hard to see stars
for lights and haze. Scraps of messages
weighing us down.

At the airport in Abu Dhabi
everyone—old, young—looked like
my father, our son.

Quick blinks—gaze away.
Write this night on the inside
of your sleeve.

We were born to wander, to grieve
lost lineage, what we did to one another,
on a planet so wide open for doing.

1935

You're 8 in the photograph,
standing behind a table of men
dipping bread in hummus.
Men on small stools
with variant headdresses,
men so absorbed in their meal
they don't see anything but food,
rough wooden table,
tiny plates,
fresh mound of bread
ripped into soft triangles.

I wish I had found this picture
while you were alive.
Did they give you the last bite?
You beam as if you owned the whole city,
could go anywhere in Jerusalem,
watch over eating with affection,
waiting your turn.

My new friend had this picture
on her wall. You spoke inside
my head the moment before I saw it.
Now the picture hangs
beside my desk, holding
layered lost worlds where
you are, not only the person I knew
but the person before the person I knew,
in your universe, your life's possible story,
still smiling.

Bats

I wrapped the dying squirrel in an old sweater.
Dry sandwich in a crackly wax sleeve.
Wrapped the crying mother inside a happy mother I made up.

Did you see that? A whirl of bats circled the yard,
everyone called them birds. The boys
were scared, but I wrapped them into my dream.

Take your large and panting dogs. I'll keep
the owl high in the eaves, a lost voice
pressed into bark of a curving oak

on the schoolyard. *My place.* Someone else's too.
Who did we think we were? *My bats.*
Live on and on. Plant things.

I wrapped the seeds in soil,
new voice in paper folded
so it looked like clothes.

I Don't Know

If my father can hear me. But it is important to pretend he can.

My sanity rests in that. The man he was can hear the daughter I am.

Scared, Scarred, Sacred

I.

Wasn't there a game, letters scrambled
how many words, make a move?

Rode a bus down Delmar, 1955
red brick buildings, shining windows,
Wizard of Oz in a theater
scared me, midgets, witches, flying house...
Coming home, sat in long back seat.

Daddy! What's that ticket
in your hand? Our transfer. For another bus
when we get off this one.
He wore a white shirt. Held the ticket tightly.
Why? Why Daddy?
Because this bus
only goes so far, then we need another one.
A different direction. We need a
different direction bus.

Why?
Because it's where we live.

I didn't want to live on that screen,
lions, scarecrows, crazy sidewalk, shiny shoes.
You'll be with me, right? I can hold your hand?
Yes, he said, watching closely, not to miss the stop.

2.

Later, he traveled everywhere, with and without us,
he felt safer traveling, wanting to be elsewhere,
restless, gone. I find stacks of pink Transfer tags in his drawer,
pulled off suitcases, but saved,
tickets to Algeria—when did you go to Algeria, Dad?—
cards, napkins with numbers.
He dreamed of doing something great
for peace, international healing,
but argued with people close by, found ways to
rumple their fur.

There's a house with a shabby yard, old man
living alone inside. On a day of great pain, my father said,
Let's go see that man. He needs us.
He wished to see a man he did not know.
The man closed the door in our faces.
No thank you. I'm fine.

Driving through garden neighborhoods
blocks from his home, blossoming streets
we'd never toured, I asked,
Have you seen these before?
He shielded his eyes. Not before and not now either.
I don't want to see them, he said.

3.

When do we get there?
That place we are going?
What have we hauled along?
It was too much, wasn't it?
Small satchel would have been sufficient.
Tucked under the seat.
All your life you were flying back to your lost life
dropping down like the Oz house.
You kept the key, as Palestinians do.
You kept the doorknocker.
And now you are homeless for real.
Fire ate your body, you became as big as the sky.

Haunted

We are looking for your laugh.
Trying to find the path back to it
between drooping trees.
Listening for your rustle
under bamboo,
brush of fig leaves,
feeling your step
on the porch,
natty lantana blossom
poked into your buttonhole.
We see your raised face
at both sides of a day.
How was it, you lived around
the edge of everything we did,
seasons of ailing & growing,
mountains of laundry & mail?
I am looking for you first & last
in the dark places,
when I turn my face away
from headlines at dawn,
dropping the rolled news to the floor.
Your rumble of calm
poured into me.
There was the saving grace
of care, from day one, the watching
and being watched
from every corner of the yard.

Valley

The ear is a purse
into which I dropped all the words I heard
on 25th Street, Ogden, Utah,
the night I knew my father would die.

Star Noodle. Still thriving?
Crossed the street for a better view.
Remembered going to the airport
to see people we didn't know departing—

of course they were also arriving, dazed and tired,
but he liked it best when they said goodbye.
I carried a lonesome person's acute cognizance of words—
"vice" suddenly tucked into "advice" making more sense.

There were places of making and toiling now boarded,
wired shut. I cried for a factory with beautiful lines.
Small city rimmed by mountains. Felt all our days
as little valleys fat with importance. Easily erased.

Still, I could not rush to his bedside
for two more days, was held and bound by clatter,
clutter, chatter, drifting around me,
the daily lives that weren't dying yet, their many pleasures.

Ordered lentil soup, small glasses of beer,
hand-brewed, for 50 cents each.
Lifted every one high. Opened a *New York Times*
on a wooden table and pressed it flat.

Storyteller

Where is the door to the story?
Is the door left open?

When he sat by our beds,
the days rushed past like water.

Driftwood, bricks,
heavy cargoes disappearing downstream,

no matter, no matter,
even the trees outside our screens

tipped their cooling leaves to listen.
We swam so easily

to the stone village,
women in thick dresses,

men with smoky breath,
we sat around the fire pitching in

our own twigs,
the world curled around us,

sizzled and popped.
We dropped our troubles

into the lap of the storyteller
and they turned into someone else's.

II

"JUST CALL ME AZIZ"
11 POEMS—TITLES BY AZIZ SHIHAB—FROM HIS NOTEBOOKS

Everything in Our World Did Not Seem to Fit

Once they started invading us.
Taking our houses and trees, drawing lines,
pushing us into tiny places.
It wasn't a bargain or deal or even a real war.
To this day they pretend it was.
But it was something else.
We were sorry what happened to them but
we had nothing to do with it.
You don't think what a little plot of land means
till someone takes it and you can't go back.
Your feet still want to walk there.
Now you are drifting worse
than homeless dust, very lost feeling.
I cried even to think of our hallway,
cool stone passage inside the door.
Nothing would fit for years.
They came with guns, uniforms, declarations.
LIFE magazine said,
"It was surprising to find some Arabs still in their houses."
Surprising? Where else would we be?
Up on the hillsides?
Conversing with mint and sheep, digging in dirt?
Why was someone else's need for a home
greater than our own need for our own homes
we were already living in? No one has ever been able
to explain this sufficiently. But they find
a lot of other things to talk about.

My Life Before America Had No Toilet Tissue

But we could stand it.
Old rags, cotton batting.
Having no justice, another matter entirely.
Having your sweet stone home
With the wrought-iron railings
Ripped out from under you
Your identity questioned
Your people's identity punched like a balloon
Connection to your own place erased by others
Very strange.
Why did they think it would work?
Would it work for you?
There were so many of us, all with the same feelings.

We Did Not Have Drinking Water
in the Middle of the Ocean

Essentially, that would be the metaphor for my entire life.
I immigrated to the land of the free,
but my people weren't free.
Tried to speak up, little droplets of words,
to a tidal wave powering over me.
Homeland trampled, ripped in pieces,
often by people who weren't there.
How dare they?
They had their own interests.
They couldn't see us.
We were tiny as pebbles to them
that you push with the toe of your shoe. What kind of people
do that? I remember the ship I came to the New World on,
how rough it was, stormy sea and sky,
deck heaving, people sick on the floors at night,
but the size of our stupid hope some mornings
as we looked across calm water and thought,
Now it will be good.

Is Misery Near Kansas, I Asked

Finding my way was a pleasure.
Every meeting a shiny maybe.
This nice lady has something to tell us.
Hello friend!
We have so much to talk about!

Many Asked Me Not to Forget Them

Where do you keep all these people?
The shoemaker with his rumpled cough.
The man who twisted straws into brooms.
My teacher, oh my teacher. I will always cry
when I think of my teacher.
The olive farmer who lost every inch of ground,
every tree,
who sat with head in his hands
in his son's living room for years after.
I tucked them into my drawer with cuff links and bow ties.
Touched them each evening before I slept.
Wished them happiness and peace.
Peace in the heart. No wonder we all got heart trouble.
But justice never smiled on us. Why didn't it?
I tried to get Americans to think of them.
But they were too involved with their own affairs
to imagine ours. And you can't blame them, really.
How much do I think of Africa? I always did feel sad
in the back of my mind for places I didn't
have enough energy to worry about.

A Kansas Preacher Called Me Muscleman

And I was a thin guy too. Such a joke!
Just call me Aziz. He wanted to change me.
As-Is. Make me stand up
to his own angel songs. I told him, Listen,
Bethlehem used to be right next door.
It was my suburb. I walked there
from home as a boy in the pack of pilgrims
burning waxy candles, at dawn. They let me trail,
opening my mouth pretending to know their words.
If you smell the skin right on my wrist here,
you'll detect the scent of rain on stones
right when you climb down those old stairs
to the church, you can come with me if you want to.
I think you can hear Jesus cry too.
And I can tell you where the secret door is,
into more than one shrine,
how far down you have to stoop to enter it.
But maybe you're too tall and thick. I don't think
you could get in there.

I Hate It, I Love It

Sometimes working at the newspaper
reading about my people's oppression,
I wanted to shred the stories instead of print them—
then take a long walk down to the Manhattan Café
and have a plate lunch with Dan who owned the place,
his people were from Greece,
ask Dan why humans are so mean to one another.
But don't you love this country? he'd say
and I'd say, Sure I do, I hate it, I love it.
He'd talk and listen, anyway, then give me
more butter for my bread.
I liked how he shrugged his shoulders
and found a smile somewhere inside
to pull out, that's what I tried to do too, especially
in my business, the news dispensing business.
It was always strange how one thing was news
and another wasn't, who's to say, or what had been
twisted by the time it reached me, also strange,
and what my mother who never heard of it might think
about any of it, sitting in her stone house with hundreds of years
in the walls, but not the real family home she loved so much,
the one we lost in Jerusalem, which we didn't talk about often,
because it was like a person who had died in another country
and we had never been able to wash the body.

When One Is So Far from Home, Life Is a Mix of Fact and Fiction

No one should hold that against you.
It's a means of survival.
Sometimes I thought my best talent was
taking a skinny story, adding wings and a tail.
Dressing it in a woolen Bedouin cloak
with stitching around the edges.
Putting a headdress on it.
Making a better picture.
Your mother got mad at me sometimes
for telling a story differently but it wasn't a lie,
just a story in different clothes
with other things emphasized.
My own mother dressed up stories for 106 years
till that last winter she rode in her bed
like a boat, sitting up to sleep.
Maybe it's our duty to be shaped
a hundred times by the same stories.
We think we're telling them
but really they're keeping us alive,
memory oxygen breathed out and in.

*Being Back with the Family Is Quite Wonderful
but Terribly Exhausting*

They always want things.
And this is the problem with family, basically.
They can't just be happy because you show up.
What's in the suitcase, what's in the pockets?
Come on, dump it.
If it's shiny it's for me.

Member of the Tribe

Unfortunately it's true.
Like it or not.
Educated or not.
This is one of the many things
Americans don't understand about Iraq.
Kill a member of the tribe,
the whole tribe now hates you.
How could they not?
The Americans think they hate you today,
thank you tomorrow.
Tribes are like tape recorders,
they won't forget. Don't ask me how
Arabs kill Arabs, knowing this.
As for Afghanistan,
I don't understand that at all.
I don't understand so many things.
Still, we must tell what we know.

Fifty Years Since I Prayed or Thought in Arabic

I was proud of my language skills.
When I was a teenager and the BBC gave me that khaki suit
to put on, with the scarf tie like a boy scout,
and stuck me in front of a microphone
big as a sunflower and handed me
the news to read, I think I was changed forever,
invisible airwaves traveling out through radios
making me feel I had something to give,
something in English, made me feel I
could travel too, visit the places news was
happening, pick it up, put it in my pocket and
pass it on. It wasn't power, it was magic.
I had a good feeling of magic walking into newspapers
for years to come, though I never spent much time
on radio again, the print voice its own magic,
but I never lost a hunger for something better to report.
I always liked the BBC even though
they couldn't save us from what happened,
no one could save us, we couldn't save ourselves,
and so long later when I was dying, it was my father's voice
I heard again for the first time since he left us,
in Arabic, as if he were standing across a bridge
talking bigger than a radio,
voice echoing over water, that familiar soft voice saying, It's fine,
you did what you could, come on now,
we're waiting.

III

Knowing

On April 16, 1953, Eleanor Roosevelt wrote a letter
to my father answering one of his own.
No, she said. I do not think Arab refugees
should be permitted to return to their homes
in Israel. There are few homes to return to.
I imagine his face, perfect burn of indignation.
He would carry his stolen home
into the next millennium and never enter it
again, though it remains intact till now.
She numbered her answers.
2. I do not know if it is advisable
to internationalize Jerusalem.
She had worked for black youth, the unemployed.
She helped to found the United Nations.
She stood up for Marian Anderson when they wouldn't
let her sing. My dad, at 25, trying to support a wife
and baby in a tired American city,
wanted to sing. Till now the same questions dangle in air.
3. I do not know if there should be an Arab Palestine
as an independent state side by side with Israel.
Very sincerely yours. She signed the letter
with a shaky hand from her perch at Val-Kill Cottage,
Hyde Park, Duchess County, New York.
Such a nice address, unencumbered
by numbers. Eleanor did not know. She was honest
about not knowing. She would die
at 78 from bone marrow tuberculosis. He would die at 80
still frustrated, still writing letters. We live on, puzzles of power
unraveling around us, building new walls, proclaiming,
protesting. One phrase worth clinging to—side by side.
My mother says he wrote her often.
This was not her only reply.

Dusk

where is the name no one answered to
gone off to live by itself
beneath the pine trees separating houses
without a friend or a bed
without a father to tell it stories
how hard was the path it walked on
all those years   belonging to none
of our struggles   drifting under
the calendar page elusive as
residue   when someone said
how have you been   it was
strangely that name that tried
to answer

Thirsty

"Israelis Kill Palestinian Boy at Protest..."

Every day the stories
say "militant"—probably
a brokenhearted boy
doing something desperate,
and I miss you. You knew.
Ahmed Moussa left too soon.
Protesting the wall
cutting off his village's olive trees
from the people who tend them,
hauling buckets of water,
the people who gather,
who sing the song of olive, all their days.
Don't go down there, begged his family.
Ten-year-old defending trees.
Who else has the patience?
Bullet in the forehead for Ahmed Moussa.
"Mourners gathered around the boy's father,
who leaned against a wall."
Morgue wall this time.
Hold them up, Dad.
From wherever you are, hold them both up.
And hold up the trees, who don't know
where their people go or how long till
they return.

Amir & Anna

It's unbelievable, this cycle of violence, and how neither party realizes they're both losing.

—Dr. Cairo Arafat, West Bank

Amir can't sleep.
He dives under his bed.
Anna is afraid of everything.
Parked cars, moving buses.
Anna is afraid of toast.
Their names begin with "A,"
contain the same number of letters.
They live one mile apart.
No one has given them
what they deserve.
Around both their houses,
all the Arab and Jewish houses,
red poppies sleep beneath
dirt and stones.
What do they know?
In March green spokes
with fluttering heads
rise and rise on every side.

Mall Aquarium, Dubai

In how many worlds are we invisible?

Blue glitter, flickering fins,
fish barely notice us
as we blur and jostle
the edges of their vision.

"The Only Democracy in the Middle East"

Please leave your house immediately.
Do not call it a home.
This is our home not yours.
Security demands it.
Always, always, security.
Our security.
Take nothing, ask nothing.
Stand over there, against the rubble, where
you belong. All young men, come with us.
You may not see your families again.
No saying goodbye or hugging.
We have suffered too much
thanks to everyone
but you are the only ones we can touch.
Don't give us any trouble.

War

If this is what we studied for,
heads bent over books in wooden desks
engraved with the names of the dead,
then I have a new feeling for
subtraction.

Olive trees, three acres slashed
equals   *zero   zero   zero.*
That's my address. The grade on my page.

If this is the spectrum of pronouns—
you kill, he or she kills, anyone might kill—
then I speak a new language without them.
Words rinse into one another recklessly—
morning, wishes, windows, paste
of kisses on a child's warm scalp.

If this is why we bow our heads to pray
in the corner, by the iron stove
so many years, forgive me.
Forget words, posture, time of day.
Blood aches inside my veins.
Where did we bury Sitti?
I will wait beside her stone,
telling the same story she told
of the river of waiting, how some of us
fall into it and are not seen again.
How some end up in another paradox
with a changed name, Mahmoud to Mo,
lost in small shops making change
for gasoline. If this is persistence,

who knows? I'm stuck in the corner of war
that's not even called war, pressed like a pigeon
into a twig cage, my dry eyes flaming.

Maximum Security

Vocabularies glittered in that tightly locked space.
Ways of breaking through, tunneling verbs,
compact muscular descriptives you could
hop a wall with, if only. *Try this on
your own time.* What they had—time.
And regret—*imagine if we'd known
these wide words in the streets.*
The youngest, celebrating his birthday,
sat in front, hands folded on desk,
smiling softly through apologies
to daughters, what happened on that avenue,
a train stalled outside a school,
normal days marked by sun, moon, money,
and lack of it. Finely tuned gerunds
clinking in succession.
Adjectives polished and combed.
How beautiful they were,
in their same suits, a crowd of men you knew
would help if you were falling, someone
pushed you down. How every one of us has
a hundred ways we could go wrong
and they are very close by. They opened lines
to climb out of them, past tense
more exquisite than present,
and repetition, mysterious comfort
of rolling back-to-back syllables,
when it might be better to insert
a new phrase or start over entirely,
if only, beams of light shaping the page.

Remembering William Stafford

Where are the better people we hoped
to be, in his memory?

Maybe for a moment
something glimmered,
small pieces fell together,
a ripple of current
pushed a certain boat
farther down a stream—

but was it enough?
You know the way he had,
embracing both sides
but claiming neither—
where was it now?
We were desperate for it.
What he said about the hard ways of peace?
How he lifted one eyebrow, never proclaimed?

Take the word humanity,
wrapped in delicate paper,
in contrast to good and evil,
those tricky packages.

Take the cool and friendly bombs
opposed to suicide bombs—
what bomb is not a suicide bomb?
The one they hide behind
or drop from a high place?
Good people never show their faces
when they drop their bombs.

The Burn

Such a swift lump rises in the throat when
a uniformed woman spits *Throw it away!*
and you tremble to comply wondering why
rules of one airport don't match another's,
used to carrying two Ziploc bags not just one
but your pause causes a uniformed man to approach
barking, *Is there something you don't understand?*
and you stare at him thinking
So many things, refugees marching
from one parched field to another,
rolled packs on their heads,
burn of ancestors smoldering outside stolen homes,
or you could be six again, yelled at on the playground
by a teacher who knew all the bad things you could do.
You're pressing little shampoos and face creams
firmly into a single plastic bag, he could slap you.
Sorry, so sorry, not wanting
to give up seven extra bottles of *Bliss brand*
lemon & sage soapy soap fresh-foaming shower gel
that you tipped the W houseboy into leaving
so you could pretend you live a Happy Hour life
back home, you hope she takes it out of the trash
when you turn away, obviously she needs a relaxing shower
and a stiff gin and he needs something like a long trip
into a country full of foreign soldiers and we all need
to swallow hard again so the lumps dissolve
and pressure eases and our worlds mingle kindly
and he no longer feels the gun in his back.

Strict

Trouble loves us too much, hiding in our cuffs.
Paul said, our mistakes allow people to love us.
Since he's Irish, I thought he said *mystique.*
Tiny beacons shining in the dark—
Flaw! Flaw! sang a bird no one could see.

White tents in Pakistan line up across a valley.
Does *mistake* have any bearing now?
How home can shift without warning,
and what happens then...

to a season, a job, a town,
how people go on about their business
even when they can't find it.
Dark-haired girls in blue uniforms
lined up in desks wanted school
to last longer.

In that world two kisses on the cheeks of an old man
could stagger a room, people wheeling backwards,
eyes wide, *you don't do this here.*
I wanted to run before a worse flap erupted,

more trouble, big big trouble, *you have no idea.*
You're right, I don't,
and I don't want one,
if it looks that sad.

Real Estate

Daddy picked up pamphlets at every stop.
He was looking for another home, a place
to get away to. If you lose
your first home you loved so much
you may be doomed. He bought
fifty acres, mouse-ridden house,
shabby barn. And kept looking.

My friend said when she was dying,
"We have to put on our armor of joy."
Maybe putting on another house
meant happy marriage, strong heart.
If he had a real master bedroom, he might
become a master.

Figure out what you're searching for, cul-de-sac
mature trees, sprinkler system, wooden deck
totally renovated spacious floor plan
fantastic location, gleaming hardwood floors
executive style, dramatic hilltop view...

Even in the last months when all the blood
from the haven of his olive-skinned body
cycled through a filtering machine every two days
he was thinking *hilltop view*—could he see all the way
across the ocean from there, the wrought-iron staircase,
the red-tiled roof?

Tiny Cucumbers

Grief is an ambush. You're walking along feeling fine, look down, see a leaf, and begin to weep.

—Jack Ridl

Slim specimens
the size of a pickle—
your excitement
lit up the aisle.

Happy with a salad,
cup of mint tea.
We lived that way for years,
minor days tucked one into another.
But what restlessness underground,
pit of the plum. Nothing worked out
in the homeland, came to fruition
or changed. Depressed stayed depressed.
You wouldn't use a cane though you'd
collected them for years.
"It will make me look old."
"You'll look older if you're dead."
Not true. In your last bed,
you became a sleek young man,
skin unruffled after the last horrible hour.

We want memories
compact as mounds of tiny cucumbers,
mottled green.
But they're not. They're dim hallways,
strange curvaceous aches. The years we'd do
anything to replay.
And here's a leaf in the shape of an "A" and
I cannot go on.

Swerve

The dog Rosie who comes home
after nine days with something darker
in her eyes will not be able to say, exactly,
where she went and what she saw.
But the summer shifts into
another key for all who searched for her.
Now we know how many mournful dogs
sprawl exhausted in dirt
on streets called Riddle and Labor,
on the back curve by the ancient brewery,
how many empty houses,
wreckages, broken shelves,
cushionless sofas, lonely tracks,
and the two shirtless brothers
who sat on the tail of their truck
watching blankly as we circled
their block. How many bony cats,
smashed bottles...and the man
in a white apron who burst forth
as I coaxed his dog from a shady bush to take
a closer look, does he keep it near him
in the kitchen now? Under the swirling fan,
thinking I have my eye on it, as the unwanted dogs
limp down to the river, panting
and the next night looms.

Where Are You Now?

I position my head on the pillow
where you told your last folktale,
mixing donkey, camel, mouse,

journey, kitchen, trees,
so the story grew jumbled,
uncharacteristically long.

I listened from the other small bed
thinking, not about the story, but,
it's the last one I'll hear from this voice,

remembering two and four and six
when this voice calmed me every night,
thinking, how will I live without this voice?

At one point, you hallucinated.
Politics came in, a rare speck
of religion, even a bad nurse

you'd had at the clinic,
frustration of long illness
tangling with the tale,

Oh Dad, you've been so brave,
to which you replied,
What else can I do?

and returned to the comforting
donkey, bucket of olives,
smoke curling up from twig fire

over which anyone, a lost girl,
a wanderer, a dying man,
could warm his hands.

Archive

If you could supply, say,
the times you lost your way,
the sudden turn down Buena Vista
some summer Sunday years ago,
grandfather slicing watermelon
on upturned green wheelbarrow,
mountain of milk crates,
& the pure wave that rolled over you,
   home
though you did not know those people,
rush of tears, the way you pulled
to the side of the road—

this might add to the archive.
You kept the rumpled maps of Alaska,
circles on Bethel & Nome,
those hard & icy working days,
the list of your students in Hawai'i
who rarely smiled,
café names sketched into margins,
old gloves smelling of wood-smoke,
faded floral shirts,
& the single thin sheet from Elizabeth Bishop
in which she spoke of the room
in which we are all waiting & waiting.
High school journals smelling of squirrel urine
(why not more care with things),
& the giant headline NEVER ENDING
that you clipped & pinned to your wall...
a business card in blue block lettering
Bassam's Fabric Store, Old City Jerusalem.

Is he safe, is he suffering,
what about suffering, could we add that
to the archive please?
A dose of midnight anguish,
wandering through rooms
after long flights,
feeling the switches' easy code.
What about carpenters, layers of tile,
plumber with his belt of wrenches,
everyone who built the rooms you slept in,
all part of an archive,
ghost signs of every city
fading on brick walls above our heads,
how they helped us navigate
even if the stores closed long ago
and there are no Easy Terms.

Won't You Still Love Me When I'm Dead?

That stopped the room.
Then, Yes! Yes!
Impossible to arrange your pillows
any comfortable way.
Tangled sheets, lives going on outside.
Where else could we have taken you?
On your last day we left for a walk,
needing orange flowers, green leaves.
You refused final dinner tray.
Ate a small can of hummus from my purse.
Everything hurt by then.
Electric lines buzzed with birds.
You called your old friend, said goodbye.
I turned my back to check e-mail.
Who was I hoping to hear from?
You were right there. Cracking
thunder the moment you left.
We'll still love you when we're dead too.

Hello, Palestine

In the hours after you died,
all the pain went out of your face.
Whole governments relaxed
in your jaw line.
How long had you been away
from the place you loved best?
Every minute was too much.
Each year's bundle of horror stories.
more trees chopped,
homes demolished,
people gone crazy.
You'd turn your face
away from the screen.
At the end you spoke
to your own blood
filtering through a machine.
We'll get there again, friend.
When you died, your long frustration
zipped its case closed.
Everyone in a body is chosen
for trouble and bliss.
At least nothing got amputated, I said
and the nurses looked quizzical.
Well, if only you had seen his country.

For Aziz, Who Loved Jerusalem

A city trades prisoners, erects blockades,
people bulldoze homes and cars, buses explode,
back and forth, the army's roaring tanks
are never called terrorists.

Three religions buried inside a city's walls.
Some kiss the walls.
Some walk beside them, emptied of belief.

My father dies with two languages
tucked inside his head.
Now we will never learn Arabic.
For half a century we lived in mighty proximity
to the resonant underpinnings,
consonants and vowels.

Now, a seven-pound box of ashes.
After many months, we still
have not scattered or buried them.
They are not him, but I kiss the box.

Undone

The workmen closed our street and sidewalk with striped yellow
sawhorses. They noisily drilled up all four corner curbs. Their
faces focused, intent on the task. They poured wet cement—
raking, smoothing to damp slopes. Cement mixer rumbled and
churned—six men, two days of work. Everyone detoured around
them.

I could easily have gone out with a nail at sunset to engrave a
moon and star in one corner of the blank gray slab, and even if
no one else noticed the fresh cement had been inscribed, I would
have known, every time I rode my bike down the smooth slope
to the old gray street you once crossed on two feet.

It makes me glad I never had to push a wheelchair with you in it
down that slope.

Could have written your name, made a heart nearly too tiny to
see—metal nail file, ice pick, needle-nose pliers, stick. Those
were the days I paused, so stunned, in the middle of everything,
as the shock swept over me.

How could you leave your desk?
Telephone numbers in your black notebook, battered briefcase,
cup of unsharpened pencils, your pens that never wrote very
well, your little Post-it pads? Marc, the nice librarian, his number
inked on top of the pad. The last number you ever wrote. Mom
cancelled your cell phone two days after you died. I could not
believe this. What if you had called us?

Love You   Love You   Love You

Still on the message machine
your triple lilt
tucked between chatter of friends
trill a sacred mark
on the wall of the cave
I stand in the light
blinking

Sandhill Cranes at the Platte River

Under their wild landing cries—
echoes the cry you made
before you died

Something far, full of horizon—
how can they sound so lonely
with all the flock around them?

Rest, now

Gray wings wheeling toward icy water

bellies full of corn

IV

This year, I'll write with ash.
Next year, peaches.

Pale yellow butterfly
darts among charred
manzanita stalks.

And the story, the story it tells?
Is yellow.

Alive

Dear Abby, said someone from Oregon,
I am having trouble with my boyfriend's attachment
to an ancient gallon of milk still full
in his refrigerator. I told him it's me or the milk,
is this unreasonable? Dear Carolyn,
my brother won't speak to me
because fifty years ago I whispered
a monkey would kidnap him in the night
to take him back to his true family
but he should have known it was a joke
when it didn't happen, don't you think?
Dear Board of Education, no one will ever
remember a test. Repeat. Stories,
poems, projects, experiments,
mischief, yes, but never a test.
Dear Dog Behind the Fence, you really need
to calm down now. You have been barking every time
I walk to the compost for two years
and I have not robbed your house. Relax.
When I asked the man on the other side
if you bother him too, he smiled and said no,
he makes me feel less alone. Should I be more
worried about the dog or the man?

Moment

To the woman who handed over
a folded note, *I have enough time*
—on a thin slip of pinkish paper,
no name or address—you're first
in mind this January 1.
Where did we meet?
You smiled shyly, stepped away.
Do you pass that note often?
Was it a singular moment?
Maybe you're a friend dropping lines
when you detect a listener.
And what am I?
There's a fine soup
to be made of every minute.
A way to stand and stir
so no one catches what you're doing.
And there's a sea of gloom
so close under the skin
that loves the taunt of a crisp new year.
Here, this fresh morning
and every to follow,
cabinet of stacked white
bowls, shines wide and plenty.
Each square of calendar
opens its hungry mouth.

The Young Poets of Winnipeg

scurried around a classroom papered with poems.
Even the ceiling, pink and orange quilts of phrase...
they introduced one another, perched on a tiny stage
to read their work, blessed their teacher who
encouraged them to stretch, wouldn't let their parents
attend the reading because parents might criticize,
believed in the third and fourth eyes, the eyes in
the undersides of leaves, the polar bears a thousand miles north,
and sprouts of grass under the snow. They knew their poems
were glorious, that second-graders could write better
than third or fourth, because of what happened
on down the road, the measuring sticks
that came out of nowhere, poking and channeling
the view, the way fences broke up winter,
or driveways separated the smooth white sheets
birds wrote on with their feet.

What Will Happen?

The honeybee and monarch,
whose lives are much shorter than ours,
hover briefly in flowers
that don't have much to offer.

Making distinctions may be more helpful
than any great talent. Knowing which way
to turn at corners, that little compass needle
tipping inside your head.

Wrap a few words around your waist—*persistence,
resilience*—where some wear passports.

Don't worry too much, what job you will have.
Alberto said, Work on what you love,
your needs will be met.

No test can measure anything important.

On the bulletin board at the San Francisco Zen Center,
someone is looking for "an unobtrusive person"
whose first duty every morning will be to make coffee.

This could be you.

Morning Birds

Crisscrossing watery tumble of sound
soothing summer drought
still they find one another   not sky
nor another parched night
can separate or silence them

*

You saw your mother
running down stairs in a dream
Would you follow her?
Absence makes no sense
You're more present than the men I see
tell me anything
please

*

What you wanted and didn't get
Is it eased now?
Someone leaves
space in a drawer
empty hangers clattering
field of mind shimmers
what never arrived
keeps us walking everywhere
we have to

bow down to what you planted
glossy figs filling bowls
sweetest rebuke to battle and bomb
all the ruins humans make

I'm open for clues   slip of straw in a beak
crane high in a tree
wing unfurled to shade her young

Lying While Birdwatching

Yes   Yes

  I see it

so they won't keep telling you

     where it is

Where Were We?

I could go anywhere now

(you are not at the end of any journey)

This evening seems open for talking

(final fold of a day)

Who do we check up on?

No ladder no map no roundabout
But a need to reach by climbing

And here are the elements we recognized,
doing nothing helpful—windows,
bare trees, tables, telephone wires.

Dear Mediator

I had a terrible night.
You won't believe what was happening.
A lion was biting my face.
Scratching my cheeks with its big paws.
I called to your father for help.
He was sitting across the room.
I don't know where the lion came from.
Help! Help! I cried.
Your father didn't move.
He stared in that vague way he had.
Get him off me!
He just sat there.
The lion was growling.
The lion was about to do further damage.
Honey I know he's been dead two years
But I have to divorce your father.

Eye Contact with a Squirrel

It changes everything—the loneliness of the tree
 where we buried Daddy's ashes—only part of them—
   perhaps his brain—or dear right hand.
 Everything moves with such regular frisk
 in the altered world—jasmine twist of spring—
   4 yellow iris on a stalk—he gave me that bulb—
I carried it in my purse—
      it never bloomed before—now boom.

      For all who lost jobs last week,
here's a day that feels like a hollowed-out tree.
   Where do you sleep, buddy-bud?
   You leap for leftover applesauce cake
         no one else will eat.

I want to say: we're all richer than we ever were,
having stared into so much, memory becomes
the Dark Ages, we're older than Lincoln
when he died. Help us, squirrelly-boy.
      We hum for scraps of language.

It's impossible to close a drawer. Trucks roar past.
On I-70 in Missouri, a FedEx truck in front of us
flipped—all the boxes flew out, popped open.
Radio drone—sin was mentioned—and I wanted some.

Family Love

Someone says, I am going
into my closet. Leave me
out of it. It is
Your Turn. I wish you
the stony cliffs at the Pecos River
and no bridge to get across.
Then you will know how I feel.

It is not a story. Stop telling me
it is a story. Yesterday I was
buying groceries and I couldn't
remember what I had at home,
it seemed I had everything
already but I knew there
was something I needed.

You Are Wanted in the Office

Sometimes deep inside a cemetery
far from the man with a shovel wiping his brow
lucent harmonies of unseen birds
blot your chaos completely.
You are clean again.
Heart in the trees, it could leave you.
Here, a huge grave for Jack and Vera,
their son in art history class
never took notes.
And—no!—a small square vault
for the ashes of Tom M.
who could not understand why
we were giving our senior class money to Peru
and called me to his desk more than once,
voice of Bad God on the crackling intercom,
you are in trouble, trouble, yes,
all your friends' faces turning toward you,
alive and in trouble, just you wait.
Hi Tom.

Dallas

The Happy 99 cent store on East Grand
is covered with black plastic. I guess
this means it burned or is closing.
As opposed to the Sad 99 cent store
which is everywhere but invisible.

I don't want anything anymore
that costs 99 cents. I already had it
and got rid of it.

Muscat Sundown

Young men erase the day's prints, raking sand.
Hundreds of netted sardines, a sheen
of final breaths hovers above waves.
Call for prayer, even the
ruffled heads of beach grass bow down.
None of the couples at this hotel
seem to speak to one another.
But they all like to read.
I'm dipped in quietude,
secret woes shimmering
inside strides and bones.
What a sweet brown country,
water so blue,
buildings low and white—
I would have loved
to walk here with you.

Burlington, Vermont

In the lovely free public library
only library I ever met
that loans out garden tools
as well as books
rakes & long-handled clippers
from large buckets by the counter
I sat in a peaceful room
with citizens I will never know
reading about far-away war
war I am paying for
war I don't want & never wanted
& put my head down
on the smooth wooden table
wishing to weep loudly or quietly
it did not matter
in the purifying presence of
women & men
shovels & hoes
devoted to growing

For Mutanabbi Street

"...books and stationery, some still tied in charred bundles, littered the street."

A single sentence which mesmerized one mind
for hours will not be seen again, in that edition,
will not be found tucked into a bookshelf
of the friend we will not meet
on the street we will not know.

What blows to pieces goes fast.
They'll give it names,
successful mission,
progress in security.

What lingers long—quiet hours reading,
in which people were the best they hadn't been yet,
something was coming,
something exquisitely new,
something anyone might do,
and the paper flicker of turning.

Mystery

The men emerge from the mine
in a cartridge with wheels
and everyone cheers.

In the hills of Afghanistan,
deserts of Gaza,
villages of Libya,
men crouching behind boulders
and broken houses
wish they knew their secret.

Endure

Mahmoud, so spare inside his elegant suit,
stepped across stony fields, bent to brush
the petal of a flower, didn't pick it.
Closed his eyes, though, holding one hand with the other,
carrying the presence of blossom back to the page.
For those who would never walk a field, never bend down,
he found a way to carry the cry of a lost goat and
the cry of a people, without stumbling.
Don't forget the streaks of tears
mapping his soft cheeks, his large and somber glasses,
the edgy poke of his thin shoulders—
how he stood a bit to the side, hand over heart,
his delicate hand on the stem of a glass,
toasting the roads and the wandering winds.
Mothers and fathers, enduring without justice,
felt his dapper presence sustaining them
though they might have found it hard to name,
the unchosen beauty of struggle and love
mixing in a fresh tonic any might drink.
His brilliance spilled in every
language, though Arabic owned him,
he became a perfect country
moving through the world, wherever he was,
and he its ruler, teacher and prophet,
he its infinite dusty workers pausing with shovels
to stare beyond the ruin they could see,
to what they will always believe in.

In Memory, Mahmoud Darwish, 1942–2008

V

Crossing the Creek

Which stone do you look at?

The one you're stepping onto
or the next?

This one's a little slick but
can't get across
without it

Later

You had time.
So much time.
And what did you do with it?
You threw it into a tunnel.
And where is it now?
Still in the tunnel.
Beneath every day you walk on.
Inside the skin of everything you touch.
No wonder a lemon feels deeper than before.
The eyes of the woman down the street follow you
because one day her husband and dog went to the park
and only the dog came back alive.
Now the tunnel is deeper
than the world you can see.
Four people called to say Henry was gone,
not one to say he was ill.
Still, you love them,
these people on top of the tunnel,
clutching little lists,
plastic tubs of summer squash
and tomatoes to share with neighbors,
or not.

Window

I'll take a Berlin tattoo
on the backside of my brain
please
but make it sound
like a train overground
long and loopy as a summer day
with three museums in it
garden paths
one burgundy peony
put a window in it
the old man who sleeps naked across the street
slope of his large cream-puff back on the bed
Last night when I couldn't sleep
I looked out the window
He was just clicking off his lamp
One hand reached back over his pink shoulder
Good dreams sir
Nothing seems strange
I love Berlin for this
love the dogs passing on a street
they seem familiar
as if they understood English
and the boys laughing on the U-train platform
Sunday afternoon
seem like the brain at rest
We went to an art show called "Locate Me"
You could put that in a tattoo
write on the top edge of a building
bending shadow of tree
thin skin of an ankle
just in case

Savigny Platz

How is it, you glitter so fiercely
in a city where you never were

poised feet at corners
hopeful daze which coats our faces

early mornings before
the little fist closes around hours

again. You would have loved
the woman with one full peachy breast

on the outside of her shirt
braless and radiant

as if she'd had too much on her mind
to button correctly or the rumpled man

lifting a beer to his lips on Saturday's train,
repeating *Nein, nein*, to every station

including the one he got off at.
I checked a blouse with tiny stars

on an outdoor rack for 5 weeks
in case the price decided to plummet

but it never did. Now I feel ashamed—
so much wasted time. The years of asking

more questions float inside
my white room's giant open windows

during Berlin's steamiest summer.
What wasn't enough,

why wasn't it?
So much pain at the end.

What else we could have done,
I didn't even bring you your *music*.

How the Israeli yesterday, after a sweet lunch together,
said to me, in Berlin of all places, *The way I see it,*

Palestinians don't even exist.
All I could say—*I wish my dad were here.*

I wish you could have known my dad.

In this brilliant city
where so many histories were scrapped,

names marked by shiny bronze plaques
in doorways, *Here lived*—

I hold Brecht's "The Doubter" to my chest
like my own second shirt, as organ grinders

toting stuffed monkeys march cheerily down Ku'Damm
wearing red suspenders and ruffles,

and gypsy accordionists hated by almost everyone
unfold their tattered cups for coins. Citizens perfecting

a stony gaze, not now, not these thinner days of the world,
but more, and layered, all the lost people,

hours, eras,
woven into sleeves and seats.

Footstool

You entered a room—
I am here, I am home.
but always a little edge—
What else, what next?
Something not arrived at.
Living here so long
with these people who were
us—what more was
needed please?
Never imagined needles,
pills, would populate your days—
after you died I collected the wrappers
of gauze pads strewn about your bed.

Trying to remember how frustrated you were
sometimes—maybe you won't mind being
disembodied so much.
Stacks of newspapers!
you'd complain, though you were the newspaper man.
If big things didn't work out—
justice and respect between countries for instance—
couldn't we just clear off the footstool
and put our feet up for awhile?
Read William Saroyan out loud, laughing—
this is exactly where I wanted to be?

Bleibtreustrasse 31

Here on Stay True Street
someone is doing something
with a large pink pipe

Someone making coffee
balancing figures on a note pad

Small dog kisses large dog
Shoes on half-price

If you order a salad
top-knot of happy sprouts

Languid motion of the young
Black shirts
Need anything?
Green apple perhaps?

How could there be war in such a world?

War in a place with such deep sun
surrounding?

Need a train to anywhere?

It is very close by

Promise

You'll have a hard time
not getting somewhere
you need to go

Last Wishes

I like it best when my side of the world is sleeping. We get into less trouble then. One might pretend the countries are peaceful, everyone reading next to a little lamp. I like the oblong pillow filled with buckwheat shells or kernels that fits right under the neck attached to a throbbing head. It makes a soft scurrying sound when adjusted. Mice in a corn crib. Something soft and normal.

When my beautiful friend age 95 asked me to help her commit suicide, I had to distract her. Tell jokes, bring up her old boyfriends...(*You know they'd put Arab in the headline...*)

My friend's problems were far greater than mine. Deeply weary of disintegrating body, dry of tongue, of eye, rich of spirit, she begged me only twice. *I will save the pills, then you...*

No!

She grinned. *Okay then. I'll suffer like a true American.*

Reciting Shakespeare loudly through the halls of that grim nursing home, heads turning her direction—what were her favorite passages?—I was soaking up the scene, how a few proud lines had power to spark nods—her English teacher's voice trumpeting through bright red lips—*old women & barns do better with a little paint!*—opening, closing, holding—the way everything changed. Language lifted us to a higher track. Sometimes before I left, in her room studded with chocolates and cards, she still talked about love affairs she wished she had had.

Ringing

I'm sorry you lost your father, people say,
and I step outside to soak
in stripes of gray cloud.
Hand touches iron rail.
You needed it, I don't.

Blood circulating under skin
and time, that blurred sky shifting.
Air holds everyone, visible or not.
Slice of lemon you craved by your teacup.
Strange affection for chipped ice.

Maybe the right wind brings
a scent of smoldering twigs,
fresh water over stone.
Maybe tonight your laughter
carpets our rooms.
I keep finding you in ways you didn't know
I noticed, or knew.

Every road, every sea,
every beach by every sea,
keeps lining up with what you loved—
Here's a line of silent palm trees.
It's as if you answered the phone.

Call to Prayer

Wish you could have died hearing these melodious sounds
instead of whatever hospital siren found you.

Wish the holy tones of the world—Buddhist gong,
cathedral bell, had lifted you from that rumpled bed

and let you know whatever
we've never been sure of.

This is what happened after you died:
women kept poking tiny cross stitches into cloth.

Kids learned every computer trick that eluded you.
Iranian missiles plundered your name.

Tehran has about 300 Shihab-3 missiles which have a range of about 900 miles.
(News Reports, 2011)

Cinco de Mayo

If this is your birthday and you are dead,
do we stay silent as the sheet
you died under? No. You always talked.
Here's a thick white candle whispering.
Pour birdseed into feeders.
Speak up, speak up.

Tell me where they go, my friend said,
in the same pain. I touched her shoulder.
Here, right here. You're closer than
you ever were—takes a while to know that.
Every scrap of DNA, he's listening.
There's a way not to be broken
that takes brokenness to find it.

Chicho Brothers Fruit & Vegetable #1

We'd sip gin at a café on the river,
pretending our lives were that fluid,
that fine. Once he said,
I'd like to see the Fruit and Vegetable place
once more. So I drove him to Laredo Street
but their store was locked. Power outage.
He said, That's how I feel, loss of power.
We drove around staring at crumbled houses,
trash heaps, pot holes. That's how I felt,
all of it. We drove back past Chicho's,
lights were on again. He stepped inside so tenderly
as if entering a shrine, placed his hand
on a mountain of grapefruit,
and bought nearly nothing because by then
he had almost no time.

Chicho Brothers Fruit & Vegetable #2

6 lemons for $1.00 said the sign.
I was thinking of you.
Absentmindedly I threw 13 lemons into a bag.
At the checkout the woman said, How many lemons?
I said, 6.
It was obvious there were more than that.
She stared at me hard.
Startled, I laughed.
They watch me closely at Chicho's now,
—cilantro, garlic, broccoli.
Come back, come back.

Frankly

No one has time for the dying.
And they don't have time for us either.
Our lunch dates and appointments,
their fitful sleeps and crusted eyes.

Students circling in a parking lot
down the road certainly don't have time.
First period coming too soon will scatter
clumps of flirtation.

Moms in fitness garb
with grocery lists and car pool numbers
stuck to refrigerators,
have too many of the living to pick up, drop off.

At the end we bore the dying,
our teary smiles, pitiful offerings.
Frank said, "If I could only get back
to my desk, back to work,"

and closed his eyes. Last line.
What a surprise to learn
the greatest pleasure of life was
all that daily labor.

Father's Day

No sadder feelings than any other day.
Every day was father's day,
mother's day,
check in to home plate
good luck to everyone day,
hoping for a lilt in the tone.
Some parents enjoyed arguing for an audience.
AA—Audiences Anonymous.
Repeat, repeat, repeat.
I used to pretend I was a drainage ditch
not a person. Then I could
absorb more. Without feeling it.
No winner, no way to cure,
no finer side of the story.
Just his weird, her weird.
Two tough breads with children stuck inside,
listening, like a trouble sandwich.
So you made things up. You had to.
Kept a rat and mouse in your bedroom,
in different cages. Sang a strange tune,
meet me under the street when night
rolls through every tunnel
and free rats and mice dance with
unfiled nails.

We Can't Lose

what we love most
    even if it dies and disappears

even if I only hear my father's voice
  when I drink a lot of rum
and walk at night on a slick wall
  over the crashing Pacific

Get back!
  Honey don't do this!
    This is not safe!

I'd say we walk a wall
every day of our lives   reaching back
for light to see by
leaning forward   baffled
how did I ever have that much motivation?
I mean—to do anything at all?

Even in Honolulu   a place
he didn't adore though they
    understood occupation
I'm seeing with the eyes he gave me
I'm a bubble in the waves

Mom Gives Away Your Ties

Just last week, nearly three years since you flew
from your miserable precious body,
I buried my face in your ties.
The dark blue Peruvian
with the little white llama.
They seemed comfortable together,
still hanging on the inside of your closet door,
mark of a man, family of shiny colors and stripes,
journalist, diplomat ties,
ties that said, *We will be hopeful
in the workplace even when we hate what we
are doing,* or *Cologne helps a man
survive,* fragrant still as your cheek
every morning of my own young world.
I thought of taking some but liked them there
in place, where you left them,
so today when I heard they'd been given
to a raggedy swap shop near a lake,
I had to stand outside a long time
in the huge air, your one real home
for all the days you walked among us.

WAR is RAW Backwards & Forwards

As my father lay dying fighting raged
   across the perfectly
      pivoted
TV screen in his hospital room

He turned his face away
   from the meal tray

waved goodbye
   to the untouched slab of beef

told us to plant his ashes
   in the ground

held a radio filled with classical music
   over his heart

     and closed his eyes

Able to Say It

So, the years go by, we find our doors and windows.
Some are always open, some never were.
Because we are stubborn, we love
the ones that won't open most.

In our first home the word "crazy" was not allowed.
So now it doubles daily, *crazy, crazy!*
Crazy we still have war on earth. Crazy bombs,
crazy ways to waste our money. Wanting people

to like us, we kill their clans to show we're stronger.
Totally crazy! When Jack was little he climbed
a tree, looked through a window onto
his own family. They were saying words

he recognized, mother, father, but he felt
the strangeness of syllables attached to knowing,
the emptiness of light and dark.
They did not know their son

was watching them so closely and he had already
disappeared, just a little, so years to come
might amplify the distance. I'd like to think
we give each other clues. You drop your notes,

someone else finds them, makes more of them
than they were even to you. Jack was brushing by
carrying everything we needed in his briefcase—
ring of keys, sack of shiny hinges,

tall folded ladder, file tabbed, "Need to Find Out."
Listening and nodding, tipping his head, mixing it up,
handing it back. If I were lost in any alley,
words from Jack could get me out. And they did.

That Boston accent which rumples
one's ear. Softened syllable, sharpened eye,
wry take on craziness that helps us live with it
even if we cannot cure, cannot fix,

are not supposed to say its name.

For Jack Myers, 1941–2009

Comfort

There's a FORT in comfort.
Sometimes hiding inside a word can help,
  subtle—well-being—book—
      two eyes, right in center.

Your favorite words still existing in the world—
  darling, coffee, friend.

When you said, What else can I do?
  else became a country of hope.

At the Red Sea a man with rolled pants
paced in water over his feet. An hour at dawn,
pausing, staring out, leaning down. What word
was he carrying? Before the sun sang
and everything went pink and gold.
Beach. Man. Turquoise.
He never looked my way.
Skittering sandpipers.
At the end of your life, only jazz
made you happy.
Shining, lonesome, day.

"Bees see your face as a strange flower."

—LiveScience.com

Nashville warblers see you as a scary-looking tree.

Garden snakes slithering into lilies see you as a storm.

The abandoned house perceives a possible doctor.

You sweep up mouse crumbs, then turn your back.

Children on the other side of the world see you as glittering.

Depressive sees your smile as a threat.

Dude playing top volume rap sees old lady staring back.

The sea, the sky, the air see us as trouble.

They're right of course. We see each other as the landmarks of a day.

History doesn't see us. It doesn't see us at all.

From this we should draw one ounce of relief.

At the Block Island Ferry

Friendly citizens poured down the ramp,
residents eager to return home
after a great storm kept them separate
from the place they love,
howling nights and extra days of waves
till the ferry ran again.
And such a blessed ferry,
big double-decked white ferry,
cheered by both sides,
those stranded on island too,
who had mostly been thinking—
let's face it—of ourselves.
In streams of families
and couples they came,
disheveled, ruddy and grateful,
in hats and winter jackets
fathers saying to daughters,
What do you need for school?
Shall we run by the house?—
lugging mainland groceries,
fishing poles, dress clothes,
some had attended a wedding,
not imagining tripled nights
away from home.
Jokes about underwear, *I'd run out!*
from people hauling ice chests, suitcases
on weary wheels, residents so ready for
their own coffee cups, pillows,
couches and books.
Their dogs had traveled too, now
sauntering onto island ground,

sniffing briskly at people, posts,
the chipper way a dog says Home.
Inside that flush of joy
my father strangely came, a sudden surge
of missing him, so sharp it caught me
by the throat.
Denied his precious land,
hounded by exile worse than waves,
he knew the grief of waiting,
years and jobs,
for a ferry's bright horn of arrival,
a ramp to be thrown down.
Who would think it?
A simple ramp! The people crossing.
At the Block Island ferry I wept for
my father, Palestine, Iraq, millions
aching for passage home,
rarely honored in their pain,
and their deaths before a ferry came—
while all around the people shouted, *Welcome back!*
It's about time!
What did you do for all those days?

Wavelength

My father didn't really cook much. But he wrote an endearing cookbook, *A Taste of Palestine*, that sold out four printings, and a year and a half after his death, my friend finds one of his last grocery lists in a red coat I'm giving away.

Does this belong to anyone? She waves it.

Tomatoes, fresh, Tomato Sauce...

His spare, classy penmanship—more printing than cursive—sears me. The frills and flourishes of his first written language, Arabic, may be evident in the "o's" and "l's" of "olive oil"—but the little white paper, folded once in half, says—I am an organized American. All hell is breaking loose in the world and in my body, but I will go to the store, buy two kinds of tomatoes and green peppers and those little baby carrots someone invented, and stir up something tasty that gives me hope again.

I must have driven him. That's why the list was in my pocket.

I'm touched by the side-note about the shrimp in the stew he grew so fond of at the end—steam, put on ice—which I misread at first as "put on rice." He was an Arab. He put many things on rice. Shrimp was not really part of his cuisine for many years. But nearing the end, in the terrible seasons of clinics and medical details, he branched out in the dining category and fell in love with a vivid one-pot dinner that he was proud to make for my mom, his children and beloved grandchildren, anyone who came by.

Pine nuts has a check mark beside it.

That must mean he already had them.

Staff of life—pine nuts. As he always had a can or two of garbanzo beans, a tub of tahini, and bulbs of garlic—staffs of life. When I was a child, he taught me how to mash up the garbanzo beans with a wooden mallet, saving a few whole ones for decorating the top of the plate of hummus with drizzled olive oil and carefully arranged marinated olives and slices of pickle. He was so happy with Arabic food.

At the end, his staff of life would have been a healthy kidney. When we're kids, he said, we hear about the heart and the brain—but look, it's the kidneys that got me! Actually, a lot of things got him. Not his brain though. Never his mind.

No doctor considered him a candidate for a transplant because his gentle heart was too weak. He'd had a quadruple bypass 19 years before and by the end, 5 stents. He didn't give up hope. He sent me racing around the back streets of Cairo to find a kidney surgeon who might, just might, give him another chance... a handsome doctor stared at me at 10 p.m. with tired eyes. "He'd never be able to withstand the drugs after surgery. His heart would not take it." Furthermore, my dad wasn't an Egyptian, and there was a law in Egypt against getting an Egyptian kidney if you weren't an Egyptian.

I could just picture it—my exiled Palestinian dad showing up in the Cairo airport with a brown paper bag and a kidney on ice...

A generally sociable guy, he tried to make the most of encounters with others during grueling dialysis rounds. He chatted with people around him, surprised they were so gloomy. They were surprised he wasn't. He felt terrible for young people on dialysis. "I hope they'll get transplants." He let technicians detail their marital problems and worried about them. Late in the evenings, before clinic days, he drove to the corner grocery to buy a big box of apple turnovers at half-price to give away to technicians the next morning. Public relations—his specialty. He had warm affection for some gay technicians who treated him most tenderly and was always slipping them fives for lunch.

Watering his lilies, a year before his last day, he said, "My time is slipping fast now."

This broke my heart, but I couldn't deny his intuition. He had been the one person in my world absolutely on my wavelength, since I was little. The one whose humor made us laugh hardest, whose quirks and commentaries rang the most bells. He sang cheerily in the shower in two languages—something better was always about to happen.

Any club or church group that invited him to talk about "growing up in the Holy Land" or "the current conflict" received an enthusiastic speaker. Nothing would have made my dad happier than to see new ground in relations between Palestinians and Israelis—his lifelong hope. Violence from any quarter frustrated him deeply. Why couldn't people talk more? Why did they give up before resolving things? Why did they spiral into violence so easily?

He'd seen enough suffering in his life—losing his Jerusalem home in 1948, traveling back and forth to the West Bank for many years to visit his resilient mother, who lived even in difficult circumstances to be 106, suffering the indignities all Palestinians suffer when visiting their precious occupied land—he chronicled his journeys in his last book *Does the Land Remember Me? A Memoir of Palestine,* which appeared in print only 4 months before his death. Thank goodness his three book-signings were sell-outs—at least he had the small gratification that some people were listening. People stood up at all his signings to thank him for telling the truth. At his first signing, he went on a bit long and I pressed a friend to cut him off—

afterward an angry woman in the crowd approached me, scolding, "You should be ashamed of yourself! He had so much more to say!"

I realize that, ma'am. I said. I was just worrying about his health. He was getting quite worked up.

He would have had more to say had he gone on ten hours.

Though never particularly religious, at the end of his days he was praying in Arabic to himself and told us he was ready to go, only twelve hours before going. He would have been stunned and amazed to see the election of President Obama—old patterns could be broken after all. He would definitely have tried to invite him to dinner.

I stand his last grocery list on my desk next to the other list I found, in which he misspelled the word "feta"—giving it two "t's"—this really surprises me. Never once was I able to beat him at Scrabble. He must have been feeling truly horrible to misspell a word.

I carry his endless stubborn hope—someday there will be justice for Palestinians and Israelis living, somehow, together. Fighting is a waste of talent. Fighting is unproductive. The United States will realize how ridiculous it is to attempt to broker peace and donate weapons to one side, at the same time.

Someday Arabs and Jews will live as the cousins, or brothers and sisters, they always were and still are. On his last night, he told us to cremate him. "You can't make him more Muslim in death than he was in life," I argued with my Arab cousins, as they lobbied us to reclaim his body from the crematorium and bury him next to a mosque.

I picked up the seven-pound box of his ashes on Halloween and kissed it, thinking of the joke he'd make. "This year, I'm dressing as ashes. Anyone recognize me?"

He loved so many people—when Marie Brenner of *Vanity Fair*, longtime writer-friend, phoned his hospital room ten minutes after he died, I placed the phone up to his cooling ear. She always told him that his words, in person and writing, had changed her own perspective about the Middle East—"as if suddenly I had taken off the sunglasses and seen facets from his unblinking eyes."

The hospital chaplain appeared at his bedside after his death and held our hands to say an ecumenical blessing for the life of a beautiful man. Then he added, "Your father really changed my perspective about the Middle East. He helped me see both sides in a more balanced way." I said, "Even when he was sick and dying? You should have met him ten years ago!" He wasn't afraid to walk the line, upset the donkey cart. His donkey, by the way, succeeded him. I regret we didn't list Yahu, the donkey, as a survivor in the obituary.

Though he had plenty of time to write us all farewell letters, he didn't. Man of words—not a goodbye peep.

My legacy. His last word. Parsley.

Acknowledgments

Ever, to Michael and Madison, their stability and steadfast kindness and deep love for Aziz. For my mother, Miriam, who bravely rocked her own world by marrying the most unusual person she had met yet, at the age of 23. Thanks to Peter Conners for his patience and to Thom Ward for early help on some of these poems. Danke forever to The Bleibtreu Hotel, Berlin, the LiteraturRaum Project, and the Lannan Foundation. Gratitude to sister and brother poets everywhere, especially Edward Hirsch, who always made my father laugh and Roberto Bonazzi, same. Thanks to Tassajara and Ryushin Paul Haller for sanity, Stu Kestenbaum and Haystack, for same, to all students, artists, teachers, librarians I have had the privilege of knowing, to precious friends and the clothes trade gang who restored the word Fun to its gleam in the lexicon. And always, listening to Tom Waits, for sound that saves.

Gratitude to magazines/journals where some of these poems first appeared: *Alhambra Calendar, Arab American Life and Culture Today, Bellevue Literary Review, Cerise Press, Five Points, Horn Book, Jung Journal, Langdon Review, Melus, The Midwest Quarterly, Nashville Review, Poet Lore, Poetry East, The Sun, The Virginia Quarterly Review,* and *World Lit Today.*

Thanks to Terry Horrigan, Protean Press, San Francisco, for the exquisite limited edition of "Endure"—2010.

About the Author

Naomi Shihab Nye lives in old downtown San Antonio, Texas, a block from the sleepy river. She has written or edited 30 previous books including *Red Suitcase*, *Fuel*, and *You & Yours* with BOA Editions, Ltd. Her collection *19 Varieties of Gazelle: Poems of the Middle East* was a finalist for the National Book Award, and her collection *Honeybee* was awarded an Arab-American Book Award. Her poetry anthologies include *Time You Let Me In*, *What Have You Lost?*, and *This Same Sky*. She is also the author of the novels *Habibi* and *Going, Going*. Her book of short-short fiction from Greenwillow Books is called *There Is No Long Distance Now*.

She is the two-time winner of the Jane Addams Book Award for Peace & Justice, and four-time winner of the Pushcart Prize. Naomi Shihab Nye is also the recipient of several fellowships, including a Lannan Fellowship, a Guggenheim Fellowship, and the Witter Bynner Fellowship from the Library of Congress.

She is currently serving on the Board of Chancellors for the Academy of American Poets.

BOA Editions, Ltd. American Poets Continuum Series

No. 1   The Fuhrer Bunker: A Cycle of
        Poems in Progress
        W. D. Snodgrass
No. 2   She
        M. L. Rosenthal
No. 3   Living With Distance
        Ralph J. Mills, Jr.
No. 4   Not Just Any Death
        Michael Waters
No. 5   That Was Then: New and
        Selected Poems
        Isabella Gardner
No. 6   Things That Happen Where
        There Aren't Any People
        William Stafford
No. 7   The Bridge of Change:
        Poems 1974–1980
        John Logan
No. 8   Signatures
        Joseph Stroud
No. 9   People Live Here: Selected
        Poems 1949–1983
        Louis Simpson
No. 10 Yin
        Carolyn Kizer
No. 11 Duhamel: Ideas of Order in
        Little Canada
        Bill Tremblay
No. 12 Seeing It Was So
        Anthony Piccione
No. 13 Hyam Plutzik:
        The Collected Poems
No. 14 Good Woman: Poems and a
        Memoir 1969–1980
        Lucille Clifton
No. 15 Next: New Poems
        Lucille Clifton
No. 16 Roxa: Voices of the Culver
        Family
        William B. Patrick
No. 17 John Logan: The Collected
        Poems

No. 18 Isabella Gardner: The Collected
        Poems
No. 19 The Sunken Lightship
        Peter Makuck
No. 20 The City in Which I Love You
        Li-Young Lee
No. 21 Quilting: Poems 1987–1990
        Lucille Clifton
No. 22 John Logan: The Collected
        Fiction
No. 23 Shenandoah and Other Verse
        Plays
        Delmore Schwartz
No. 24 Nobody Lives on Arthur
        Godfrey Boulevard
        Gerald Costanzo
No. 25 The Book of Names:
        New and Selected Poems
        Barton Sutter
No. 26 Each in His Season
        W. D. Snodgrass
No. 27 Wordworks: Poems Selected and
        New
        Richard Kostelanetz
No. 28 What We Carry
        Dorianne Laux
No. 29 Red Suitcase
        Naomi Shihab Nye
No. 30 Song
        Brigit Pegeen Kelly
No. 31 The Fuehrer Bunker:
        The Complete Cycle
        W. D. Snodgrass
No. 32 For the Kingdom
        Anthony Piccione
No. 33 The Quicken Tree
        Bill Knott
No. 34 These Upraised Hands
        William B. Patrick
No. 35 Crazy Horse in Stillness
        William Heyen
No. 36 Quick, Now, Always
        Mark Irwin

No. 37 *I Have Tasted the Apple*
Mary Crow

No. 38 *The Terrible Stories*
Lucille Clifton

No. 39 *The Heat of Arrivals*
Ray Gonzalez

No. 40 *Jimmy & Rita*
Kim Addonizio

No. 41 *Green Ash, Red Maple,
Black Gum*
Michael Waters

No. 42 *Against Distance*
Peter Makuck

No. 43 *The Night Path*
Laurie Kutchins

No. 44 *Radiography*
Bruce Bond

No. 45 *At My Ease: Uncollected Poems
of the Fifties and Sixties*
David Ignatow

No. 46 *Trillium*
Richard Foerster

No. 47 *Fuel*
Naomi Shihab Nye

No. 48 *Gratitude*
Sam Hamill

No. 49 *Diana, Charles, & the Queen*
William Heyen

No. 50 *Plus Shipping*
Bob Hicok

No. 51 *Cabato Sentora*
Ray Gonzalez

No. 52 *We Didn't Come Here for This*
William B. Patrick

No. 53 *The Vandals*
Alan Michael Parker

No. 54 *To Get Here*
Wendy Mnookin

No. 55 *Living Is What I Wanted:
Last Poems*
David Ignatow

No. 56 *Dusty Angel*
Michael Blumenthal

No. 57 *The Tiger Iris*
Joan Swift

No. 58 *White City*
Mark Irwin

No. 59 *Laugh at the End of the World:
Collected Comic Poems
1969–1999*
Bill Knott

No. 60 *Blessing the Boats: New and
Selected Poems: 1988–2000*
Lucille Clifton

No. 61 *Tell Me*
Kim Addonizio

No. 62 *Smoke*
Dorianne Laux

No. 63 *Parthenopi: New and Selected
Poems*
Michael Waters

No. 64 *Rancho Notorious*
Richard Garcia

No. 65 *Jam*
Joe-Anne McLaughlin

No. 66 *A. Poulin, Jr. Selected Poems*
Edited, with an Introduction
by Michael Waters

No. 67 *Small Gods of Grief*
Laure-Anne Bosselaar

No. 68 *Book of My Nights*
Li-Young Lee

No. 69 *Tulip Farms and Leper Colonies*
Charles Harper Webb

No. 70 *Double Going*
Richard Foerster

No. 71 *What He Took*
Wendy Mnookin

No. 72 *The Hawk Temple at Tierra
Grande*
Ray Gonzalez

No. 73 *Mules of Love*
Ellen Bass

No. 74 *The Guests at the Gate*
Anthony Piccione

No. 75 *Dumb Luck*
Sam Hamill

No. 76 *Love Song with Motor Vehicles*
Alan Michael Parker

No. 77 *Life Watch*
Willis Barnstone

No. 78   The Owner of the House: New
          Collected Poems 1940–2001
          Louis Simpson
No. 79   Is
          Wayne Dodd
No. 80   Late
          Cecilia Woloch
No. 81   Precipitates
          Debra Kang Dean
No. 82   The Orchard
          Brigit Pegeen Kelly
No. 83   Bright Hunger
          Mark Irwin
No. 84   Desire Lines: New and Selected
          Poems
          Lola Haskins
No. 85   Curious Conduct
          Jeanne Marie Beaumont
No. 86   Mercy
          Lucille Clifton
No. 87   Model Homes
          Wayne Koestenbaum
No. 88   Farewell to the Starlight in
          Whiskey
          Barton Sutter
No. 89   Angels for the Burning
          David Mura
No. 90   The Rooster's Wife
          Russell Edson
No. 91   American Children
          Jim Simmerman
No. 92   Postcards from the Interior
          Wyn Cooper
No. 93   You & Yours
          Naomi Shihab Nye
No. 94   Consideration of the Guitar:
          New and Selected Poems
          1986–2005
          Ray Gonzalez
No. 95   Off-Season in the Promised
          Land
          Peter Makuck
No. 96   The Hoopoe's Crown
          Jacqueline Osherow
No. 97   Not for Specialists:
          New and Selected Poems
          W. D. Snodgrass

No. 98   Splendor
          Steve Kronen
No. 99   Woman Crossing a Field
          Deena Linett
No. 100   The Burning of Troy
          Richard Foerster
No. 101   Darling Vulgarity
          Michael Waters
No. 102   The Persistence of Objects
          Richard Garcia
No. 103   Slope of the Child Everlasting
          Laurie Kutchins
No. 104   Broken Hallelujahs
          Sean Thomas Dougherty
No. 105   Peeping Tom's Cabin:
          Comic Verse 1928–2008
          X. J. Kennedy
No. 106   Disclamor
          G.C. Waldrep
No. 107   Encouragement for a Man
          Falling to His Death
          Christopher Kennedy
No. 108   Sleeping with Houdini
          Nin Andrews
No. 109   Nomina
          Karen Volkman
No. 110   The Fortieth Day
          Kazim Ali
No. 111   Elephants & Butterflies
          Alan Michael Parker
No. 112   Voices
          Lucille Clifton
No. 113   The Moon Makes Its Own Plea
          Wendy Mnookin
No. 114   The Heaven-Sent Leaf
          Katy Lederer
No. 115   Struggling Times
          Louis Simpson
No. 116   And
          Michael Blumenthal
No. 117   Carpathia
          Cecilia Woloch
No. 118   Seasons of Lotus, Seasons of
          Bone
          Matthew Shenoda

No. 119   *Sharp Stars*
          Sharon Bryan
No. 120   *Cool Auditor*
          Ray Gonzalez
No. 121   *Long Lens: New and Selected Poems*
          Peter Makuck
No. 122   *Chaos Is the New Calm*
          Wyn Cooper
No. 123   *Diwata*
          Barbara Jane Reyes
No. 124   *Burning of the Three Fires*
          Jeanne Marie Beaumont
No. 125   *Sasha Sings the Laundry on the Line*
          Sean Thomas Dougherty
No. 126   *Your Father on the Train of Ghosts*
          G.C. Waldrep and John Gallaher
No. 127   *Ennui Prophet*
          Christopher Kennedy
No. 128   *Transfer*
          Naomi Shihab Nye

Colophon

Transfer, poems by Naomi Shihab Nye, is set in Hoefler Text, a digital font designed for Apple Computer in 1981 by the American typeface designer Jonathan Hoefler (1970–).

The publication of this book is made possible, in part, by the special support of the following individuals:

Anonymous & Bernadette Catalana

Leaf E. Drake & Peter & Suzanne Durant

Romolo Celli & Elizabeth Forbes

Suressa & Richard Forbes

Pete & Bev French & Heidi Friederich

Anne Germanacos & Robert L. Giron

Michael S. Glaser

Suzanne Gouvernet

T. Michael Hall & William B. Hauser

Kit Abel Hawkins & Bob & Willy Hursh

Robin, Hollon & Casey Hursh, *in memory of Peter Hursh*

X. J. Kennedy

Jack & Gail Langerak & Katy Lederer

Susan Burke & Bill Leonardi, *in memory of Al Poulin,*
in honor of Boo Poulin

Deborah Ronnen & Sherman Levey

Rosemary & Lew Lloyd

Peter & Phyllis Makuck & Frances & Robert Marx

Janice N. Harrington & Robert Dale Parker

Boo Poulin,
in honor of Susan Burke & Bill Leonardi, in memory of Debra Audet
John F. Roche

Steven O. Russell & Phyllis Rifkin-Russell

Vicki & Richard Schwartz

Rob Tortorella, *in honor of Paul Tortorella*

Gerald Vorrasi, *in memory of Greg Liphard*

Ellen & David Wallack & Glenn & Helen William